Way Cool

Spanish

Phrase Book

(Second Edition)

JANE WIGHTWICK

New York Chicago San Francisco Lisbon London Madrid Mexico City
Milan New Delhi San Juan Seoul Singapore Sydney Toronto

About this book

Jane Wightwick
had the idea

Wina Gunn
wrote the pages

Leila & Zeinah Gaafar
(aged 10 and 12) drew the
first pictures in each
chapter

Robert Bowers
(aged 56) drew the
other pictures, and
designed the book

Ana Bremon
did the Spanish stuff

Important things that **must** be included

© **2009 by g-and-w** PUBLISHING

1 2 3 4 5 6 7 8 9 0   09 10 11 12

ISBN 978-0-07-161583-9
MHID 0-07-161583-0

McGraw-Hill books are available at special quantity discounts to use as premiums and sales promotions or for use in corporate training programs. To contact a representative, please visit the Contact Us pages at www.mhprofessional.com.

This book is printed on acid-free paper.
Printed and bound by Tien Wah Press, Singapore.

3

What's inside

4

Hanging out

At the pool, beach, or theme park—don't miss out on the action **70**

Pocket money

Spend it here! **90**

Grown-up talk

blah!
blah!
blah!
blah!

If you really, really have to! **100**

Extra stuff

All the handy things—numbers, months, time, days of the week **108**

Half a step this way

stepfather/stepmother
padrastro/madrastra
👄 padrastro/madrastra

stepbrother/stepsister
hermanastro/hermanastra
👄 airmanastro/airmanastra

half-brother/half-sister
medio hermano/medio hermana
👄 medyo airmano/medyo airmana

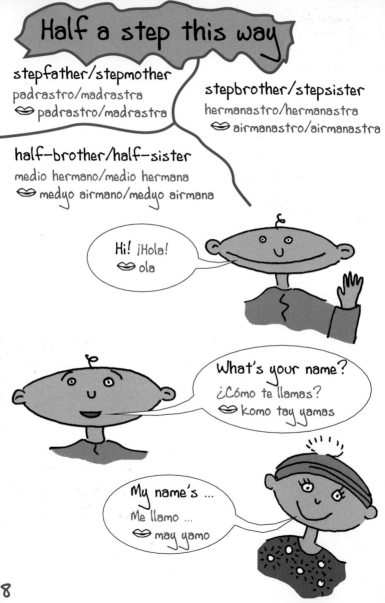

Hi! ¡Hola!
👄 ola

What's your name?
¿Cómo te llamas?
👄 komo tay yamas

My name's ...
Me llamo ...
👄 may yamo

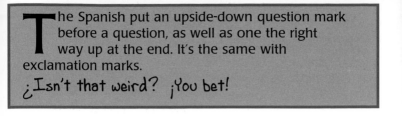

The Spanish put an upside-down question mark before a question, as well as one the right way up at the end. It's the same with exclamation marks.

¿Isn't that weird? ¡You bet!

9

from Canada
de Canadá
👄 day canadah

from Ireland
de Irlanda
👄 day eerlanda

from Scotland
de Escocia
👄 day escosya

from Wales del País de Gales
👄 del pie-yis day gal-les

That means "the land of the Gauls"

from the U.S.
de los Estados Unidos
👄 day los estados
    ooneedos

from England
de Inglaterra
👄 day eengla-tairra

Los textos

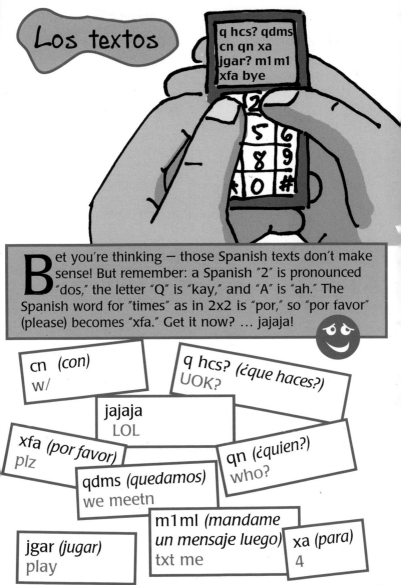

q hcs? qdms
cn qn xa
jgar? m1m1
xfa bye

B et you're thinking — those Spanish texts don't make sense! But remember: a Spanish "2" is pronounced "dos," the letter "Q" is "kay," and "A" is "ah." The Spanish word for "times" as in 2x2 is "por," so "por favor" (please) becomes "xfa." Get it now? … jajaja!

cn (con)
w/

q hcs? (¿que haces?)
UOK?

jajaja
LOL

xfa (por favor)
plz

qn (¿quien?)
who?

qdms (quedamos)
we meetn

m1m1 (mandame
un mensaje luego)
txt me

xa (para)
4

jgar (jugar)
play

Star signs

AQUARIUS
Jan. 21 – Feb. 19
Acuario ❤ akwaree-o

PISCES
Feb. 20 – Mar. 20
Piscis ❤ pees-thees

ARIES
Mar. 21 – Apr. 20
Aries ❤ a-rees

TAURUS
Apr. 21 – May 21
Tauro ❤ towro

GEMINI
May 22 – June 21
Géminis ❤ hemeenees

CANCER
June 22 – July 23
Cáncer ❤ kansair

LEO
July 24 – Aug. 23
Leo ❤ leo

VIRGO
Aug. 24 – Sep. 23
Virgo ❤ beergo

LIBRA
Sep. 24 – Oct. 23
Libra ❤ leebra

SCORPIO
Oct. 24 – Nov. 22
Escorpio ❤ eskorpee-o

SAGITTARIUS
Nov. 23 – Dec. 21
Sagitario ❤ sa-heetaree-o

CAPRICORN
Dec. 22 – Jan. 20
Capricornio ❤ kapreecornee-o

14

soccer el fútbol
👄 el footbol

rollerblading el patinaje en línea
👄 el patee-nahay en leenya

music la música
👄 la mooseeka

electronic games los juegos electrónicos
👄 los hway-gos elektroneekos

tv la tele
👄 la taylay

comics los tebeos
👄 los taybayos

spiders las arañas
👄 las aranyas

school el colegio
👄 el kolay-heeyo

School

15

What's your ...?
¿Cuál es tu ...?
👄 kwal es too ...

favorite group
grupo preferido
👄 groopo prefereedo

favorite color
color preferido
👄 kol-lor prefereedo

Page 69

favorite game
juego preferido
👄 hway-go
prefereedo

favorite food
comida preferida
🗣 komeeda prefereeda

favorite ring tone
tono preferido
🗣 tone-oh prefereedo

favorite animal
animal preferido
🗣 anee-mal prefereedo

favorite team
equipo preferido
🗣 ekeepo prefereedo

Talk about your pets

He's hungry
Está hambriento
👄 esta ambree-yento

She's sleeping
Está durmiendo
👄 esta doormee-yendo

Can I pet your dog?
¿Puedo acariciar a tu perro?
👄 pwedo asaree-syar ah too pair-ro

Do you have any pets?
¿Tienes alguna mascota?
👄 tee-enes algoona mascota

dog el perro
🗣 el pair-ro

cat
el gato
🗣 el gato

snake
la serpiente
🗣 la serpee-entay

guinea-pig la cobaya
🗣 la kob-eye-a

hamster
el hámster
🗣 el hamstair

budgie
el periquito
🗣 el peree-keeto

My little doggy goes *guau guau!*

A Spanish doggy (that's "guauguau" in baby language) doesn't say "woof, woof," it says *"guau, guau"* (*gwa-oo, gwa-oo*). A Spanish bird says *"pío, pío"* (*pee-o, pee-o*) and "cock-a-doodle-do" in Spanish chicken-speak is *"kikirikí"* (*kee-kee ree-kee*). But a cat does say *"miaow"* and a cow *"moo"* whether they're speaking Spanish or English!

19

Talk about school (if you can stand it)

geography
la geografía
👄 la heogra-feeya

PE
la gimnasia
👄 la heem-naseeya

art
el dibujo artístico
👄 el deebooho
arteesteeko

math las matemáticas
👄 las matay-mateekas

Spanish
m.smith
form 2b

Spanish
el español
👄 el espanyol

music
la música
👄 la mooseeka

English
el inglés
👄 el eeng-les

science
las ciencias
👄 las see-en-see-as

history
la historia
👄 la eestoreeya

IT
TI
👄 tay-ee

School rules!

In Spanish-speaking countries many children have to wear a uniform to school and discipline is often strict. On the other hand, they enjoy long vacation breaks: about 10 weeks in the summer and another 5–6 weeks during the school year. But before you turn green with envy, you might not like the mounds of **"tareas para las vacaciones"** (*taray-as para las bakasee-yones*), that's "vacation homework"! And if you fail your exams, the teachers could make you repeat the whole year with your little sister!

Gossip

Can you keep a secret?
¿Puedes guardar un secreto?
👄 pwedes gwardar oon sekreto

Do you have a boyfriend (a girlfriend)?
¿Tienes novio (novia)?
👄 tee-enes nobyo (nobya)

An OK guy/An OK girl
Un chavo bueno/ Una chava buena
👄 oon chabo bwayno/ oona chaba bwayna

Way bossy!
¡Qué mandón!
👄 kay man-don

He/She's nutty!
¡Está como una cabra!
👄 esta komo oona kabra
That means "He/She's like a goat"!

"I'm not like that at all!"

What a complainer!
¡Qué malasombra!
👄 kay malas-sombra

You won't make many friends saying this!

Bug off!
¡Vete a la porra!
👄 betay a la porra

Shut up! ¡Cállate!
👄 kigh-yatay

If you're fed up with someone, and you want to say something like "you silly …!" or "you stupid …!", you can start with **_"pedazo de"_** (which actually means "piece of …") and add anything you like. What about …

Stupid banana!
¡Pedazo de plátano!
(pedaso day platano)

or …

Silly sausage!
¡Pedazo de salchicha! *(pedaso day salcheecha)*

Take your pick. It should do the trick. You could also try **_"¡pedazo de idiota!"_** *(pedaso day eedee-ota)*. You don't need a translation here, do you?

25

Stop it!
¡No hagas eso!
👄 no agas eso

I want to go home!
¡Me quiero ir a casa!
👄 may kyairo eer ah kassa

I don't care
Me da igual
👄 may da eegwal

At last!
¡Por fin!
👄 por feen

27

Saying goodbye

Here's my address
Aquí tienes mi dirección
👄 akee tee-enes mee
    deerek-syon

What's your address?
¿Cuál es tu dirección?
👄 kwal es too deerek-syon

Come to visit me
Ven a visitarme
👄 ben a
    beesee-tarmay

Have a good trip!
¡Buen viaje!
👄 bwen bee-ahay

Write to me soon
Escríbeme pronto
👄 eskree-bemay pronto

Send me a text
Envíame un text
👄 envee-armay oon "text"

Shall we chat online?
¿Chateamos?
👄 chatay-amos

Bye!
¡Adiós!
👄 adeeyos

What's your email address?
¿Cuál es tu mail?
👄 kwal es too mail

♫□@3◇*@ℛ.com

WANNA PLAY?

el elástico
👄 el elasteeko

el ping-pong
👄 el "ping-pong"

el reproductor
👄 el raypro-dooktor

el celular
👄 el saylyoolar

el yo-yó
👄 el "yo yo"

WANNA PLAY?

Do you want to play ...?
¿Quieres jugar ...?
👄 keyair-res hoogar

... foos-ball?
... al futbolín?
👄 al footboleen

... cards?
... a las cartas?
👄 a las kartas

... on the computer?
... con el ordenador?
👄 kon el orden-ador

... tic-tac-toe?
... a las tres en raya?
👄 a las trays en righ-ya

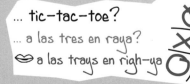

33

Fancy a game of **foal** or **donkey**?!

In Spain, you don't play "leap frog", you play "foal" – *el potro*. There is also a group version of this called "donkey" – *el burro*. This involves two teams. Team 1 line up in a row with their heads down in the shape of a donkey. Team 2 take it in turns to leap as far as they can onto the back of the "donkey". If the donkey falls over, Team 2 win. If Team 2 touch the ground or can't leap far enough to get all the team on, then Team 1 win – got that?! Spanish children will try to tell you this is enormous fun, but your parents might not be so happy about the bruises!

Can my friend play too?

¿Mi amigo también puede jugar?

👄 mee ameego tam-byen pway-day hoogar

I have to ask my parents

Se lo tengo que pedir a mis papás

👄 say loe tengo kay pedeer ah mees pa-pas

Who dares?

You're it!
¡La quedas tú!
👄 la kedas too

Race you?
¿Una carrera?
👄 oona karraira

I'm first
Soy el primero (boys)
Soy la primera (girls)
👄 soy el preemairo
soy la preemaira

Who's winning? ¿Quién gana?
👄 keeyen gana

Ready, steady, go!
En sus marcas, listos, ¡fuera!
👄 en soos markas, leestos
fwairah

Where's the finish?
¿Dónde está la meta?
👄 donday esta la mayta

I need a head start
Necesito ventaja
👄 naysay–seeto benta–ha

37

Electronic games

la pantalla
👄 la pan-tie-ya

el módem
👄 el "modem"

el CD-Rom
👄 el say-day rom

el ratón
👄 el rat-ton

el teclado
👄 el teklado

el micro
👄 el meek-ro

los cascos
👄 los kas-kos

Show me
Enséñame
 ensay–nyamay

Am I dead?
¿Me han matado?
may an matado

What do I do?
¿Qué hay que hacer?
kay eye kay asair

Shoot–em–up!
¡Dispárales!
deespar–ralayz

How many lives do I have?
¿Cuántas vidas tengo?
kwantas beedas tengo

How many levels are there?
¿Cuántos niveles hay?
kwantos neebay–les eye

39

It's virtual fun!

Do you have a webcam?
¿Tienes una cámara web?
👄 tee-enes oona kam-ara web?

Send me a message.
Mándame un mensaje.

How do i join?
¿Cómo me apunto?

I'm not old enough.
No tengo edad suficiente.

I'm not allowed.
No tengo permiso.

I don't know who you are.
No te conozco.

My profile

my blog
mi blog
👄 mee blog

my friends
mis amigos
👄 mees ameegos

my photos
mis fotos
👄 mees fotos

my videos
mis videos
👄 mees bee-dayos

my music mi música
👄 mee mooseeka

41

hockey
el hockey
👄 el "hockey"

gymnastics
la gimnasia
👄 la heem-nasya

basketball el baloncesto
👄 el ballon-sesto

ballet
el ballet
👄 el ballay

and, of course, we haven't forgotten *"el fútbol"* … (P.T.O.) 43

soccer

cleats
las botas
👄 las botas

football gear
el equipo de fútbol
👄 el ekeepo day footbol

ref
el árbitro
👄 el arbeetro

shin-pads
las espinilleras
👄 las espinee-yeras

Good save!
¡Vaya parada!
👄 baya parada

Pass! ¡Pasa! 👄 pasa

46

Keeping the others in line

Not like that!
¡Así no!
👄 asee no

You cheat!
¡Tramposo! (boys only)
¡Tramposa! (girls only)
👄 tramposo/tramposa

I'm not playing anymore
Ya no juego
👄 ya no hwego

Stop it!
¡No hagas eso!
👄 no agas eso

It's not fair!
¡No es justo!
👄 no es hoosto

47

Showing off

... do a handstand?
... hacer el pino?
👄 asair el peeno

Can you ... ¿Sabes ...
👄 sabays

Look at me!
¡Mírame!
👄 meera-may

... do a cartwheel?
... dar volteretas laterales?
👄 dar boltair-retas latairal-les

... do this?
... hacer esto?
👄 asair esto

Impress your Spanish friends with this!

You can show off to your new Spanish friends by practising this tongue twister:

Tres tristes tigres comían trigo en un trigal.
trays treestays teegrays comee-an treego en oon treegal
(This means "Three sad tigers ate wheat in a wheat field.")

Then see if they can do as well with this English one:
"She sells seashells on the seashore, but the shells she sells aren't seashells, I'm sure."

For a rainy day

deck of cards
una baraja de cartas
👄 oona baraha
 day kartas

my deal/your deal
yo doy/tú das
👄 yo doy/too das

king
el rey
👄 el ray

queen
la reina
👄 la ray-eena

jack
la jota
👄 la hota

joker
el komodín
👄 el komodeen

tréboles
👄 trebol-les

corazones
👄 korazon-nes

picas
👄 peekas

diamantes
👄 dee-amantays

Do you have the ace of swords?!

Y ou might also see children playing with a different deck of cards. There are only 48 cards instead of 52 and the suits are also different. Instead of clubs, spades, diamonds and hearts, there are gold coins (*oros*), swords (*espadas*), cups (*copas*) and batons (*bastos*).

chessboard
el tablero
👄 el tablairo

el alfil
👄 el alfeel

el peón
👄 el pay-on

el rey 👄 el ray

la reina
👄 la ray-eena

el caballo
👄 el kab-eye-o

la torre 👄 la torray

51

Grub

I'm starving

Tengo un hambre de lobo

👄 tengo oon ambray day lobo

That means "I have the hunger of a wolf!"

el lobo

Please can I have ...

Por favor, me da ...

👄 por fabor, may da

... a croissant
... un cruasán
👄 oon krwasan

... a cream pastry
... un bollo con nata
👄 oon boyo kon nata

... a sweet roll
... una palmera
👄 oona palmayra

... a waffle
... un wafle
👄 oon wah-flay

... a muffin
... una magdalena
👄 oona magda-layna

los churros
 👄 los choorros

These are wonderful sugary donut-like snacks. They are sold in cafés and kiosks and usually come in a paper cone. They are also very popular for breakfast in winter, with thick hot chocolate (***chocolate con churros***).

You: Can I have some churros, Mom?

Mom: No. They'll make you fat and rot your teeth.

You: But I think it's good to experience a foreign culture through authentic local food.

Mom: Oh, all right then.

Churros? *"¡Mm, mm!,"* Garlic sandwich? *"¡Agh!"* If you're going to make foody noises you'll need to know how to do it properly in Spanish!

"Yum, yum!" is out in Spanish. You should say *"¡Mm, mm!."* And "Yuk!" is *"¡Agh!"* (pronounced "ag"), but be careful not to let adults hear you say this!

... **a lemonade**
una limonada
👄 oona leemon-
    adah

I n Mexico and other countries the 'Limondas' are carbonated. So instead of a plain lemonade, you're actually getting a lemon or lime soda-pop.

... **water** agua
👄 agwa

... **a milkshake**
... un batido de leche
👄 oon bateedo day lechay

Y ou get your hot chocolate in a large cup (to dunk your churros in).

... **a hot chocolate**
... un chocolate
👄 oon chokolatay

Adventures in eating!

If you're travelling in Mexico and Central America and you don't like hot spicy food, a good question to know if "*¿Es picante?*" (*es peekantay* – "Is it spicy?"). If the answer is no, your tongue won't catch on fire!

And if you're hungry for comfort food, you can ask for one of the following dishes:

noodle soup

sopa de fideos

👄 sopa day feeday-os

spaghetti

espaguetis

👄 espaghetees

... with meatballs

con albóndigas

👄 kon albon-deegas

and there's always...

pizza

pizza

👄 peessa

Parties

balloon el globo
👄 el glow-bo

Can I have some more?
¿Me puedes dar más?
👄 may pwedays dar mas

party hat
el gorro de fiesta
👄 el gorro day fee-esta

This is for you
Esto es para ti
👄 esto es para tee

LOOKING GOOD

tank top
el top
🗣 el "top"

bracelets
las pulseras
🗣 las poolsairas

belt
el cinturón
🗣 el seen-
tooron

shorts
los pantalones
cortos
🗣 los panta-
lone-nes kortos

ballet flats
las zapatillas de ballet
🗣 las zapa-teeyas
day ballay

leg warmers
los calientapiernas
🗣 los kaleeyenta-
peeyairnas

That T-shirt please
Esa camiseta, por favor
🗣 esa kameeseta, por fabor

Cool tattoo!
¡Qué calcamonía más padre!
🗣 kay kalka-moneeya mass padray

The pink frilly one
La rosa con volantitos
🗣 la rosa kon bolanteetos

Awesome miniskirt!
¡Vaya minifalda mas chula!
🗣 baya meenee falda
mass choola

The purple striped one
La morada de rayas
🗣 la morada day righ-yas

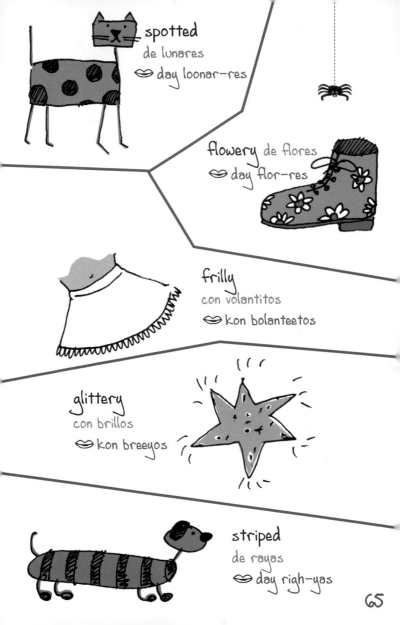

spotted
de lunares
👄 day loonar-res

flowery de flores
👄 day flor-res

frilly
con volantitos
👄 kon bolanteetos

glittery
con brillos
👄 kon breeyos

striped
de rayas
👄 day righ-yas

Clothes

jeans
los vaqueros
👄 los
bakayros

sweatshirt
la sudadera
👄 la sooda-
dayra

T-shirt
la camiseta
👄 la kameeseta

soccer jersey
la camiseta de fútbol
👄 la kameeseta day footbol

tennis shoes
las deportivas
👄 las daypor-teebas

shoes los zapatos
👄 los sapatos

66

skirt
la falda
👄 la falda

dress
el vestido
👄 el bay-
steedo

pants
los pantalones
👄 los panta-
lone-nes

A pair of cowboys?

The word for jeans in Spanish (*los vaqueros* – *los bakayros*) actually means "cowboys" because they were the first people to wear these pants.

Make it up!

lip gloss
el Brillo de labios
👄 el breeyo day labyos

glitter gel
la brillantina
👄 la breeyan-teena

nail polish
el barniz de uñas
👄 el barnees day oon-yas

earrings los aretes
👄 los aray-tays

I need a mirror
Necesito un espejo
👄 netsayseeto oon espay-ho

eye shadow
la sombra de ojos
👄 la sombray day o-hos

Can you lend me your flat iron?
Me prestas tu alisador de pelo? 👄 may pray-stas too alee-sadoor day pay-lo

68

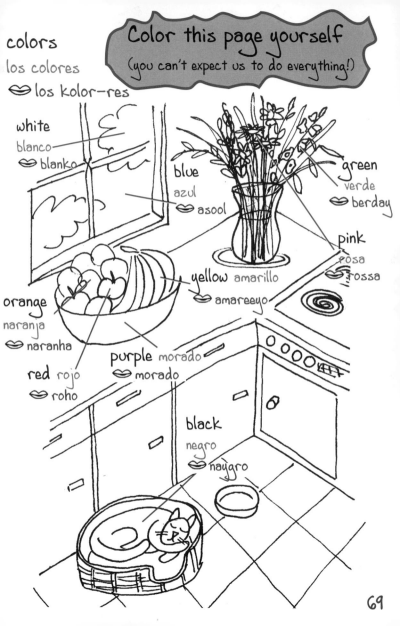

colors
los colores
👄 los kolor-res

white
blanco
👄 blanko

blue
azul
👄 asool

green
verde
👄 berday

pink
rosa
👄 rossa

yellow amarillo
👄 amareeyo

orange
naranja
👄 naranha

purple morado
👄 morado

red rojo
👄 roho

black
negro
👄 naygro

69

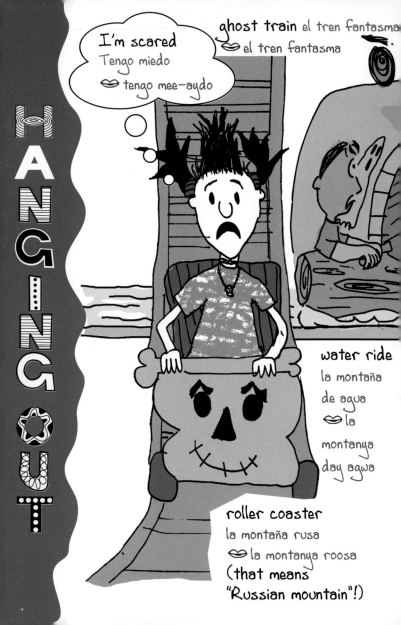

What should we do?
¿Qué hacemos?
👄 kay asay-mos

Can I come?
¿Puedo ir?
👄 pwedo eer

Where do you all hang out?
¿Por dónde salen ustedes?
👄 por donday salen oos-tedays

That's mega!
¡Qué emoción!
👄 kay aymosee-yon

I'm (not) allowed
(No) me dejan
👄 (no) may day-han

Let's go back Regresemos
👄 regray–saymos

That gives me goose bumps (or "chicken flesh" in Spanish!)
Eso me pone la carne de gallina
👄 eso may ponay la karnay day gayeena

I'm bored to death
Me muero de aburrimiento
👄 may mwero day aburree–mee–ento

HOUSE OF MIRRORS

That's a laugh
Te ríes cantidad
👄 tay reeyes kanteedad

73

sea el mar
👄 el mar

beach
la playa
👄 la playa

sandcastle
el castillo de arena
👄 el casteeyo day arayna

towel
la toalla
👄 la toe-aya

bathing suit
el bañador
👄 el banyador

snorkel
el tubo
👄 el toobo

bucket el cubo
👄 el koobo

shovel
la pala
👄 la palla

shells
las conchas
👄 las konchas

It's going swimmingly!

How to make a splash in Spanish!

PLOF

Let's hit the swimming pool
Vamos a la piscina
👄 bamos a la peeseena

Can you swim (underwater)?
¿Sabes nadar (debajo del agua)?
👄 sabays nadar (debaho del agwa)

Me too/ I can't
Yo también/Yo no
👄 yo tambeeyen/ yo no

Can you dive?
¿Te sabes tirar de cabeza?
👄 tay sabays teerar day kabaysa

I'm getting changed
Me estoy cambiando
👄 may estoy kambee-ando

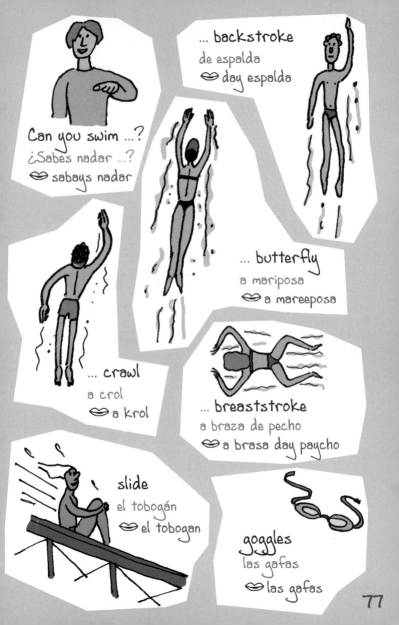

Can you swim ...?
¿Sabes nadar ...?
👄 sabays nadar

... backstroke
de espalda
👄 day espalda

... butterfly
a mariposa
👄 a mareeposa

... crawl
a crol
👄 a krol

... breaststroke
a braza de pecho
👄 a brasa day paycho

slide
el tobogán
👄 el tobogan

goggles
las gafas
👄 las gafas

77

Downtown

Pooper-scoopers on wheels!

In Spain, you might see bright green-and-white motorcycles with funny vacuum cleaners on the side riding around town scooping up the dog poop. The people riding the bikes look like astronauts! (Well, you'd want protection too, wouldn't you?)

Do you know the way?
¿Sabes el camino?
😊 sabays el kameeno

Let's ask
Vamos a preguntar
😊 bamos a pray-goontar

bus
el autobús
😊 el owtoboos

Is it far? ¿Está lejos?
👄 esta lay-hos

car el coche
👄 el kochay

Are we allowed in here?
¿Nos dejan entrar aquí?
👄 nos day-han entrar akee

You can show off your "street-smarts" to your new Spanish friends by using some slang. A junky old car is *"una cafetera"* (*oona cafaytayra*), which means "coffee pot"! Try this: *"¡Vaya cafetera!"* (*baya cafaytayra* – "What an old clunker!").

79

Park yourself here

swings los columpios
👄 los koloom-peeyos

jungle gym
el juego para escalar
👄 el hway-go para eska-lar

playground
el patio de recreo
👄 el pateeyo day rekrayo

grass la hierba
👄 la yairba

tree el árbol
👄 el ar-bol

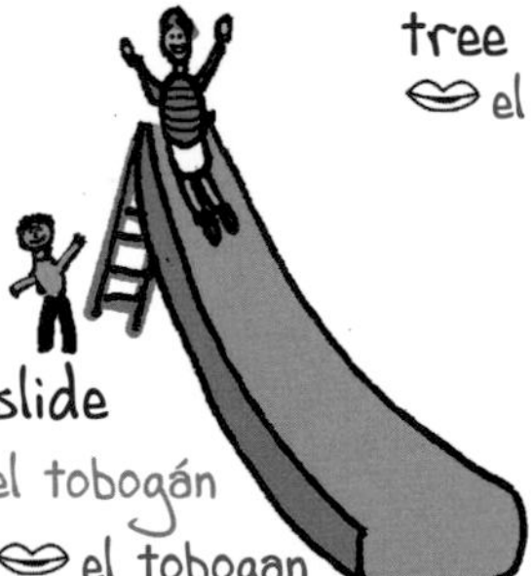

slide
el tobogán
👄 el tobogan

park el parque 👄 el parkay

Can we play ball games?

¿Podemos jugar a la pelota?

poday-mos hoo-gar a la pay-lota

merry-go-round

el carrusel

el kar-roosel

sandbox el arenero

el arain-airo

Can I have a go?

¿Puedo intentarlo?

pwaydo intain-tarloe

81

Picnics

I hate wasps
Odio las avispas
👄 odeeyo las abeespas

Move over!
¡Apártate!
👄 apar-tatay

bread el pan
👄 el pan

Shall we sit here?
¿Nos sentamos aquí?
👄 nos sentamos akee

napkin
la servilleta
👄 la serbeeyeta

ham el jamón
👄 el hamon

cheese
el queso
👄 el kayso

yohurt
el yogur
👄 el yogur

chips
las papas fritas
👄 las papas freetas

drinks
las bebidas
👄 las bebeedas

knife
el cuchillo
👄 el koocheeyo

spoon
la cuchara
👄 la koochara

fork
el tenedor
👄 el tenaydor

wasps
las avispas
👄 las abeespas

bees
las abejas
👄 las abayhas

bzzzz

ants
las hormigas
👄 las ormeegas

Wake up, campers!

tent la tienda
👄 la tyen-da

tent peg la piqueta
👄 la pee-kayta

camper van
la caravana
👄 la kara-vana

penknife
la navaja de bolsillo
👄 la nava-ha day
bol-seelyo

camping stove
la estufa portátil
👄 la aystoofah porta-teel

sleeping bag el saco de dormir
👄 el sak-ko day door-meer

flashlight la linterna
👄 la lintair-na

That tent's a palace!
¡Esa tienda es un palacio!
👄 esa tyen-da es oon palass-yoh

Is there a campfire?
¡Hay una hoguera?
👄 ay oona og-waira

I've lost my flashlight
Perdí mi linterna
👄 pairdee mee lintair-na

The showers are gross
¡Las regaderas están asquerosas!
👄 las raiga-dairas están askairosas

Where does the rubbish go?
¿Dónde se tira la basura?
👄 donday say teera la basoora

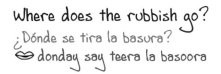

85

All the fun of the fair

slide
el tobogán 👄 el tobogan

Ferris wheel
la noria
👄 la noreeya

house of mirrors
la casa de los espejos 👄 la kasa day los espayhos

bumper cars
los coches de choque 👄 los kochays day chokay

Shall we go on this?
¿Nos montamos en éste?
👄 nos montamos en estay

merry-go-round
el pulpo
👄 el poolpo

It's very fast
Va muy rápido
👄 ba mwee rapeedo

That's for babies
Eso es para los pequeños
👄 eso es para los pekay-nyos

Do you get wet in here?
¿En éste te mojas?
👄 en estay tay mohas

I'm not going on my own
Yo solo no me monto
👄 yo solo no may monto

87

Disco nights

mirror ball
la bola de espejos
👄 la bola day
espay-hos

loudspeaker
el altavoz
👄 el altab-oss

Can I request a song?
¿Puedo pedir una canción?
👄 pwaydo paydeer oona kan-syon

The music is really lame
¡La música es malísima!
👄 la mooseeka es malee-seema

DJ
el pinchadiscos
👄 el peencha-
deeskos

spotlights
los focos
👄 los fo-kos

turntable
el tocadiscos
👄 el toka-deeskos

PAY

How old do I need to be?
¿Cuántos años tengo que tener?
👄 kwantos anyos tengo kay tenair

dance floor
la pista de baile
👄 la peesta day balay

Let's dance!
¡Vamos a bailar!
👄 ba-mos a balar

I love this song!
¡Me encanta esta canción!
👄 may enkanta esta kan-syon

89

POCKET MONEY

candy
los caramelos
👄 los karamaylos

T-shirts
las camisetas
👄 las kameesetas

toys los juguetes
👄 los hoogaytays

el tendero
👄 el tendayro

books
los libros
👄 los leebros

el móvil
👄 el mobeel

pencils los lápices
👄 los lapeeses

POCKET MONEY

What does that sign say?

Carnicería

carnicería
butcher shop
👄 karneesereeya

pastelería
cake shop
👄 pasteler
—reeya

Pastelería

panadería
bakery
👄 panadereeya

Panadería

confitería
candy store
👄 confeeter-
reeya

Verdulería

papelería
office supplies
👄 papelereeya

PAPELERÍA

verdulería
**fruit and
vegetable store**
👄 berdoolereeya

boutique
clothes shop
👄 booteek

Boutique

Sweet heaven!

I love this shop
Me encanta esta tienda
👄 may enkanta esta tee-enda

Let's get some sweets
Vamos a comprar chucherías
👄 bamos a comprar choochereeyas

Let's get an ice-cream
Vamos por un helado
👄 bamos por oon aylado

lollipops las piruletas
👄 las peerooletas

a bar of chocolate
una tableta de chocolate
👄 oona tableta day chokolatay

chewing gum el chicle
👄 el cheeklay

If you really want to look cool and end up with lots of fillings ask for:

regaliz (regaleess)
soft licorice sticks, available in red or black

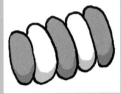

nubes (noobes)
soft marshmallow candies in different shades (**nubes** means clouds)

jamones (hamon-nes)
fruity, fizzy gums in the shape of hams ("ham" is **jamón**)

Chupa-chups® (choopa-choops)
lollies famous all over the world, but they come from Spain

polvos pica-pica (polvos peeka peeka)
tangy fizzy sherbet sold in small packets with a lollipop to dip in

kilométrico (keelomay-treeko)
chewing gum in a strip like dental floss – pretend to the adults that you're flossing your teeth!

Other things you could buy

(that won't rot your teeth!)

What are you getting?
¿Qué te vas a comprar?
👄 kay tay bas a komprar

That toy, please
Ese juguete, por favor
👄 esay hoogetay, por fabor

Two postcards, please
Dos postales, por favor
👄 dos postal-
les, por fabor

This is garbage
Esto es una porquería
👄 esto es oona
porkayreeya

This rules!
¡Chévere!
👄 chay-bairay

I'm getting ...

Voy a comprar
👄 boy a comprar

... a pen
... un boli
👄 oon bolee

... stamps
... sellos
👄 seyos

... felt tip pens
... rotuladores
👄 rotoolador-res

... colored pencils
... lápices de colores
👄 lapeeses day kolor-res

lápices de colores

... a key ring
... un llavero
👄 oon yabairo

... comics
... tebeos
👄 taybayos

97

... a fridge magnet
... un imán del refri
👄 oon ee-man del ray-free

... a shell box
... un joyero de conchas
👄 oon ho-yairo day konchas

How much is that?
¿Cuánto cuesta?
👄 kwanto kwesta

... a CD
... un compact
👄 oon compact

For many years Spain's favorite comics have been *Mortadelo y Filemón*, two accident-prone TIA agents (<u>not</u> CIA) and *Zipi y Zape*, two very naughty twins. Children also like to read *Mafalda*, an Argentinian comic, *Carlitos y Snoopy* (Charlie Brown & Snoopy), *Tintin*, *Astérix* and *¿Dónde está Wally?* (Where's Waldo?).

Money talks

How much pocket money do you get?
¿Cuánto te dan para gastos?
🗩 kwanto tay dan para gastos

I only have this much
Sólo tengo esto
🗩 soul-lo tain-go esto

Can you lend me 10 pesos?
¿Me prestas diez pesos?
🗩 may praystas deeyes paysos

No way!
¡Ni hablar!
🗩 nee ablar

Money talk

Money varies in the different Spanish-speaking countries:

Spain = **euro** (*ay-ooro*)

Mexico = **peso** (p*aysoh*)

Guatemala = **quetzales** (*ketsalays*)

Costa Rica = **colones** (*kolonays*)

But if you're in Puerto Rico, you're all set – the money is U.S. dollars!

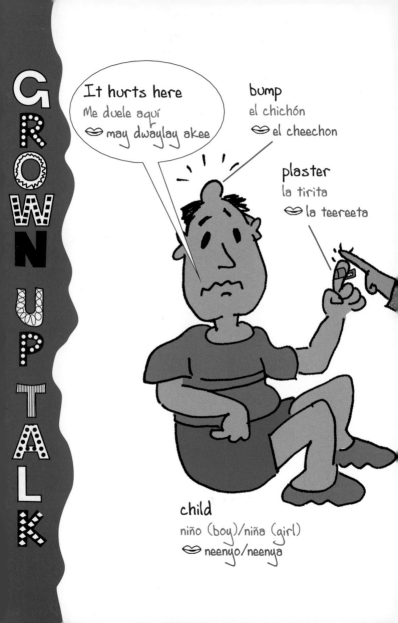

Help!

Something has dropped/broken
Algo se ha caído/roto
👄 algo say a kigh-eedo/roto

Please
Por favor
👄 por fabor

Can you help me?
¿Me puedes ayudar?
👄 may pwedes ayoodar

Where's the mailbox?
¿Dónde está el buzón?
👄 donday esta el booson

Where are the toilets?
¿Dónde están los aseos?
👄 donday estan los asayos

I can't manage it
No puedo
👄 no pwedo

Could you pass me that?
¿Me pasas eso?
👄 may pasas eso

What's the time?
¿Qué hora es?
👄 kay ora es

Come and see
Ven a ver
👄 ben a bair

May I look at your watch?
¿Me deja que mire su reloj?
👄 may deha kay meera soo reloh

103

Lost for words

... my ticket
mi billete
👄 mee beeyaytay

I've lost ...
He perdido ...
👄 eh perdeedo

... my cell phone
mi celular
👄 mee saylyoolar

... my parents
mis padres
👄 mees padrays

... **my shoes**
mis zapatos
👄 mees sapatos

... **my money** mi dinero
👄 mee deenayro

... **my sweater**
mi suéter
👄 mee sweatair

... **my watch**
mi reloj
👄 mee reloh

... **my jacket** mi chaqueta
👄 mee chakayta

105

ADULTS ONLY!

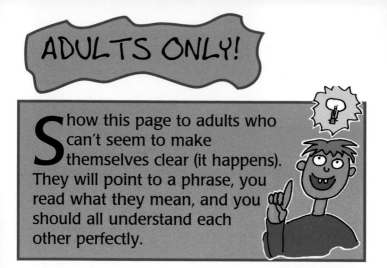

Show this page to adults who can't seem to make themselves clear (it happens). They will point to a phrase, you read what they mean, and you should all understand each other perfectly.

No te preocupes
Don't worry

Siéntate aquí
Sit down here

¿Tu nombre y apellidos?
What's your name and surname?

¿Cuántos años tienes?
How old are you?

¿De dónde eres?
Where are you from?

¿Dónde te alojas?
Where are you staying?

¿Dónde te duele?
Where does it hurt?

¿Eres alérgico a algo?
Are you allergic to anything?

Está prohibido
It's forbidden

Tiene que acompañarte un adulto
You have to have an adult with you

Voy por alguien que hable inglés
I'll get someone who speaks English

weather
el tiempo
el tyem-po

numbers los números
los noo-mairos

time
la hora
👄 la ora

EXTRA STUFF

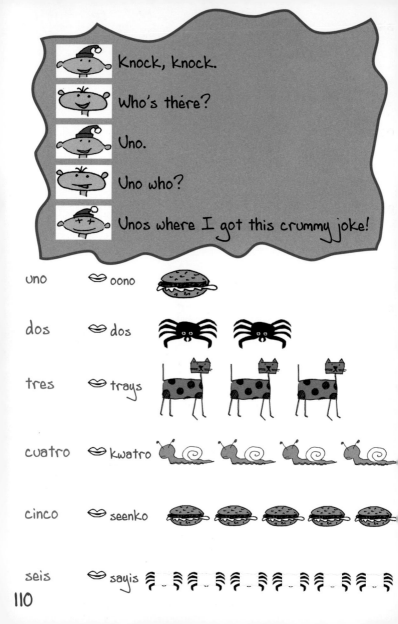

Knock, knock.

Who's there?

Uno.

Uno who?

Unos where I got this crummy joke!

uno 👄 oono

dos 👄 dos

tres 👄 trays

cuatro 👄 kwatro

cinco 👄 seenko

seis 👄 sayis

110

siete ✎ see-etay

ocho ✎ ocho

nueve ✎ nwebay

diez ✎ deeyess

once ✎ onsay

doce ✎ dosay

trece 👄 tresay

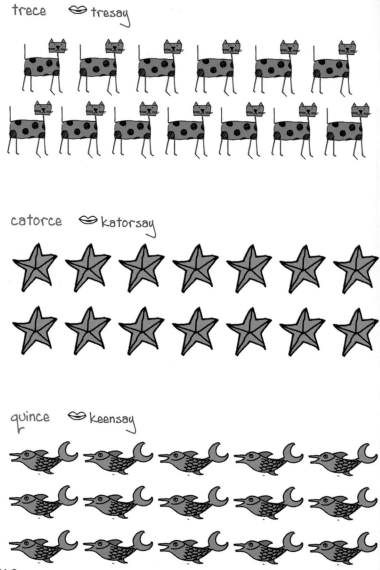

catorce 👄 katorsay

quince 👄 keensay

16	dieciséis	*deeyesee sayis*
17	diecisiete	*deeyesee see-etay*
18	dieciocho	*deeyesee ocho*
19	diecinueve	*deeyesee nwebay*

If you want to say "twenty-two," "sixty-five," and so on, you can just put the two numbers together like you do in English. But don't forget to add the word for "and" (**y**, pronounced *ee*) in the middle:

32	**treinta y dos**	*traynta ee dos*
54	**cincuenta y cuatro**	*seenkwenta ee kwatro*
81	**ochenta y uno**	*ochenta ee oono*

20	veinte	*baintay*
30	treinta	*traynta*
40	cuarenta	*kwarenta*
50	cincuenta	*seenkwenta*
60	sesenta	*saysenta*
70	setenta	*saytenta*
80	ochenta	*ochenta*
90	noventa	*nobenta*
100	cien	*seeyen*

1,000 mil *meel*

a million *un millón* *oon meel-yon*

a gazillion! *chorrocientos!* *chorroh-seeyentos*

1st	primero	*preemairo*
2nd	segundo	*segoondo*
3rd	tercero	*tersayro*
4th	cuarto	*kwarto*
5th	quinto	*keento*
6th	sexto	*sexto*
7th	séptimo	*septeemo*
8th	octavo	*octabo*
9th	noveno	*nobayno*
10th	décimo	*dayseemo*

Want a date?

If you want to say a date in Spanish, you don't need to use 1st, 2nd, etc. Just say

Lunes	Martes	Miércoles	Jueves	Viernes	Sábado	Domingo
		1	2	3	4	5
6	7	8	9	10	11	12
13	14	15	16	17	18	19
20	21	22	23	24	25	26
27	28	29	30			

the ordinary number followed by *de* (*day*):

uno de marzo   (1st of March)

diez de julio   (10th of July)

March	marzo	*marso*
April	abril	*abreel*
May	mayo	*my-yo*

June	junio	*hooneeyo*
July	julio	*hooleeyo*
August	agosto	*agosto*

September	septiembre	*septee-embray*
October	octubre	*octoobray*
November	noviembre	*nobee-embray*

December	diciembre	*deesee-embray*
January	enero	*enayro*
February	febrero	*febrayro*

primavera *preemabayra*

verano *berano*

otoño *otonyo*

FALL

invierno *eenbee-erno*

118

Monday	lunes	*loon-nes*
Tuesday	martes	*mar-tes*
Wednesday	miércoles	*mee-erkol-les*
Thursday	jueves	*hoo-ebes*
Friday	viernes	*bee-er-nes*
Saturday	sábado	*sabado*
Sunday	domingo	*domeengo*

By the way, many kids have a two-and-a-half hour lunch break! Time enough for lunch and a siesta. But school doesn't finish until 5pm.

Good times

It's ...
Son ...
👄 sonn

(five) o'clock
las (cinco)
👄 las (seenko)

quarter after (two)
las (dos) y cuarto
👄 las (dos) ee kwarto

quarter to (four)
las (cuatro) menos cuarto
👄 las (kwatro) menos kwarto

half past (three)
las (tres) y media
👄 las (trays) ee medya

five after (ten)
las (diez) y cinco
👄 las (deeyess) ee
seenko

twenty after (eleven)
las (once) y viente
👄 las (onsay) ee
baintay

ten to (four)
las (cuatro) menos diez
👄 las (kwatro) menos
deeyess

twenty to (six)
las (seis) menos veinte
👄 las (sayis) menos
baintay

Watch out for "one o'clock." It's a little different from the other times. If you want to say "It's one o'clock" you have to say **Es la una** (*es la oona*). "It's half past one" is **Es la una y media** (*es la oona ee medya*), and so on.

121

morning
mañana
👄 la manyarna

midday mediodía
👄 el medyo-deeya

afternoon la tarde
👄 la tarday

evening la noche
👄 la nochay

midnight
la medianoche
👄 la medya-nochay

122

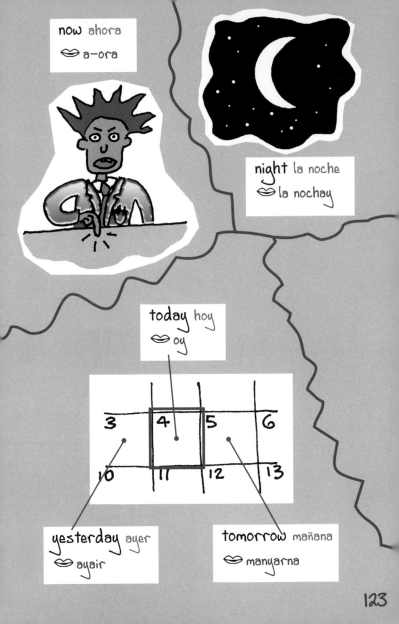

123

Weather wise

It's hot
Hace calor
👄 asay kalor

Can we go out?
¿Podemos salir fuera?
👄 podaymos saleer fwera

It's cold
Hace frío 👄 asay freeyo

It's a horrible day
Hace un día horrible
👄 asay oon deeya orreeblay

It's raining seas!

In Spanish it doesn't rain "cats and dogs", it rains "seas"! That's what they say when it's raining really heavily:
¡Está lloviendo a mares!
esta yobeeyendo a mar-res